SCHOLASTIC

File-Folder Games in COLOR
Social Studies

by **Immacula A. Rhodes**

New York • Toronto • London • Auckland • Sydney
Mexico City • New Delhi • Hong Kong • Buenos Aires

Teaching *Resources*

To my brother and sisters

"Be joyful in hope, patient in affliction, faithful in prayer."

— ROMANS 12:12

Cover design by Jason Robinson
Interior design by Solas
Cover and interior illustrations by Rusty Fletcher

ISBN-13: 978-0-439-51763-8
ISBN-10: 0-439-51763-X

1 2 3 4 5 6 7 8 9 10   40   16 15 14 13 12 11 10 09

Contents

File-Folder Games

About This Book

File-Folder Games in Color: Social Studies offers an engaging and fun way to motivate children of all learning styles and help them build vocabulary and essential reading skills while reinforcing social studies skills and concepts. Research shows that repetition and multiple exposure to content-area words and concepts enhance vocabulary development and comprehension. The games in this book are also designed to help children meet important curriculum standards. (See Meeting the Social Studies and Language Arts Standards, page 6, for more.)

The games are a snap to set up and store: Just tear out the full-color game boards from this book, glue them inside file folders, and you've got ten instant learning center activities. Children will have fun learning as they explore a variety of places with the game Inside-Out Community, match quotations to workers in Career Talk, learn about how goods get to market in Heigh-Ho, The Dairy-O!, identify holiday and seasonal signs and symbols in Super Seasons, Special Times!, and much more.

What's Inside

Each game includes the following:

- an introductory page for the teacher that provides a suggestion for introducing the game

- Step-by-step assembly directions

- Extending the Game activities to continue reinforcing children's skills and interest

- a label with the title of each game for the file-folder tab

- a pocket to attach to the front of the file folder for storing the game parts

- directions that explain to children how to play the game

- an answer key

- game cards

- one or more game boards

- some games also include game markers and a game cube, number pyramid, or spinner

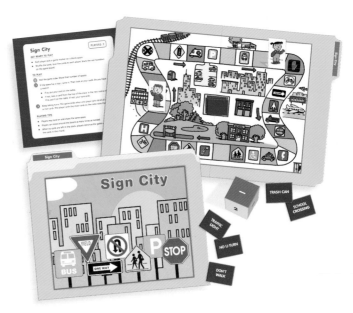

Making the File-Folder Games

In addition to the game pages, you will need the following:

- 10 file folders (in a variety of colors, if possible)
- scissors
- clear packing tape
- glue stick or rubber cement
- paper clips
- brass fasteners

Tips

- Back the spinners, game cubes, number pyramids, and game markers with tagboard before assembling. Laminate for durability.

- Before cutting apart the game cards, make additional copies (in color or black and white) for use with the Extending the Game activities.

- Place the accessories for each game, such as spinners, game cubes, number pyramids, and game markers in separate, labeled zipper storage bags. Keep the bags in a basket near the games.

Using the File-Folder Games

- Before introducing the games to children, conduct mini-lessons to review the social studies vocabulary and concept used in each game.

- Model how to play each game. You might also play it with children the first time.

- Give children suggestions on how to determine the order in which players take turns, such as rolling a die and taking turns in numerical order.

- Store the games in a learning center and encourage children to play in pairs or small groups before or after school, during free choice time, or when they have finished other tasks.

- Send the games home for children to play with family members and friends.

- Use the Extending the Game activities to continue reinforcing children's skills and interest.

Storage Ideas

Keep the file-folder games in any of these places:

- learning center
- vertical file tray
- file box
- file cabinet
- bookshelf
- plastic stacking crate

What the Research Says

In an effective early social studies curriculum, vocabulary development is essential to building the knowledge base needed for learning and understanding social studies concepts. In fact, the important relationship between vocabulary and reading comprehension extends across all content areas. In its review of reading research, the National Reading Panel concluded that effective strategies for building children's vocabulary include direct and indirect instruction, repeated meaningful exposure to new words, and rich and varied contexts for learning. Children learn content-area vocabulary best from a combination of teaching methods, including purposeful interaction with the related concepts.

Meeting the Social Studies and Language Arts Standards

Connections to the McREL Social Studies and Language Arts Standards

Mid-continent Research for Education and Learning (McREL), a nationally recognized, nonprofit organization, has compiled and evaluated national and state standards—and proposed what teachers should provide for their students to grow proficient in language arts and social studies, among other curriculum areas. The games and activities in this book support the following standards:

SOCIAL STUDIES

Civics
- Understands rules and the purposes they serve
- Understands the concept of fairness
- Knows that a responsibility is a duty to do or not do something
- Knows examples of situations that involve responsibility; and some of the benefits of fulfilling responsibilities
- Knows how different groups in the community take responsibility (e.g., police, fire department)

Economics
- Knows that people in the community have different jobs and responsibilities
- Knows that goods are objects that can satisfy people's wants, and services are activities that can satisfy people's wants

Geography
- Knows common features (street signs, roads, buildings) found in the local environment
- Knows natural features of the environment (hills, mountains, oceans, rivers)
- Knows the physical and human characteristics of the local community (neighborhoods, schools, parks, shopping areas, airports, museums, hospitals)

History
- Understands family life today and how it compares with family life in the recent past and long ago
- Understands reasons important figures were significant to our democracy
- Understands ways in which people have advanced the cause of human rights and equality
- Understands the reasons that Americans celebrate certain national holidays
- Knows the history of American symbols (the eagle, Liberty Bell, national flag) and why important buildings, statues, and monuments are associated with national history
- Knows the accomplishments of major scientists and inventors

LANGUAGE ARTS
Uses the general skills and strategies of the reading process:
- Uses mental images based on pictures and print to aid in comprehension of text
- Uses meaning clues to aid comprehension and make predictions about content
- Understands level-appropriate sight words and vocabulary
- Uses self-correction strategies

Sources: National Reading Panel. (2000). *Teaching children to read: An evidence-based assessment of the scientific research literature on reading and its implications for reading instruction: Report of the subgroups* (NIH Publication No. 00–4754). Washington, DC: National Institute of Child Health and Human Development.

Kendall, J. S. & Marzano, R. J. (2004). *Content knowledge: A compendium of standards and benchmarks for K–12 education.* Aurora, CO: Mid-continent Research for Education and Learning. Online database: http://www.mcrel.org/standards-benchmarks/

Social Studies Vocabulary and Concepts

The following lists show the social studies vocabulary and concepts used in each file-folder game:

Blue Ribbon Citizens
(*citizenship*)

Tell the truth.
Stay in line.
Say "please."
Say "thank you."
Use the trash can.
Follow the rules.
Use kind words.
Recycle paper and cans.
Wait your turn to speak.
Return library books.
Clean up after yourself.
Share your toys.
Cross a street carefully.
Use hand signals on your bike.
Donate to the food bank.
Visit elderly friends.
Help at the animal shelter.
Walk away from fights.
Talk out problems.
Help keep the park clean.
Say nice things to a friend.
Use an indoor voice.
Be polite to others.
Listen and follow directions.

Inside-Out Community
(*places in the community*)

airport, bank, clothing store, dentist's office, doctor's office, fire station, grocery store, hospital, library, movie theater, museum, park, pet store, police station, post office, restaurant, school, shoe store, toy store, zoo

Career Talk
(*community helpers*)

artist, builder, bus driver, cashier, chef, custodian, dentist, doctor, dry cleaner, firefighter, florist, hair stylist, letter carrier, librarian, meteorologist, plumber, police officer, secretary, teacher, veterinarian

Sign City
(*common signs in the community*)

Airport, Ambulance, Bicycle Crossing, Bus Stop, Do Not Enter, Don't Walk, Fire Department, Handicapped Parking, Hospital, No Bicycles, No U-turn, One Way, Parking, Pedestrian Crossing, Police Department, Railroad Crossing, School Crossing, Stop, Telephone, Traffic Light, Trash Can, U.S. Mail, Walk, Yield

Go, Go, Go! (*transportation*)

airplane, ambulance, bicycle, blimp, bus, car, elevator, helicopter, horse, hot-air balloon, in-line skates, motorcycle, pedestrian, pushcart, rowboat, RV, sailboat, scooter, ship, skateboard, stroller, subway, taxi, train, truck, tugboat, van, wagon, wave runner, wheelchair

Heigh-Ho, the Dairy-O!
(*how goods get to market*)

The farmer grows grain.
Cows eat the grain.
Cows go to the milking parlor.
Cows are milked twice a day.
Milk is put in a special truck.
The milk is heated.
Some milk is put in containers.
Some milk is used for dairy foods.
Products go to a supermarket.
The products are put out to sell.
Shoppers buy the products.
Kids enjoy the products at home.

Super Seasons, Special Times!
(*holiday and seasonal signs and symbols*)

Fall: first day of school, harvest, Hispanic Heritage Month, Columbus Day, Halloween, Thanksgiving

Winter: Hanukkah, Christmas, Kwanzaa, New Year's Day, Chinese New Year, Valentine's Day

Spring: St. Patrick's Day, Passover, Easter, Earth Day, Mother's Day, Memorial Day

Summer: Flag Day, Father's Day, 4th of July, summer vacation, picnic, baseball

All-American Museum
(*historical figures and symbols of America*)

4th of July, Abraham Lincoln, Alexander Graham Bell, American Flag, Bald Eagle, Cesar Chavez, Clara Barton, George Washington, George Washington Carver, Harriet Tubman, Liberty Bell, Martin Luther King, Jr., Mayflower, Orville and Wilbur Wright, Sally Ride, Squanto, Statue of Liberty, Susan B. Anthony, U.S. Capitol, White House

America, Past and Present
(*comparing past and present lifestyles*)

Past: hand-made clothing, open-flame cooking, hand-picked corn, horse-drawn wagon, candlelight, marbles and box, quill and parchment, small home with thatched-roof, self-caught fish, homemade straw doll, homemade bread, horse-drawn plow

Present: store-bought clothing, microwave oven, store-bought canned corn, automobile, electric lamp, electronic game, computer, large home with shingled roof, store-bought fish, factory-made plastic doll, store-bought bread, motorized tractor

Great Eight State Park
(*mapping natural landforms*)

cave, hill, island, lake, mountain, river, swamp, waterfall

Blue Ribbon Citizens

PLAYERS: 2

SKILL

This game provides practice in recognizing traits that make a good citizen.

INTRODUCTION

Help students create a list of traits that describe good citizens. (You may wish to use the balloons on the game board as a reference.) Then invite them to tell about times when they personally demonstrated good-citizen traits or observed others being good citizens.

ASSEMBLING THE GAME

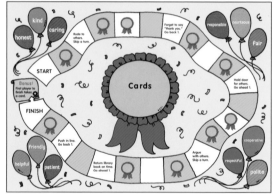

1 Remove pages 9–19 from the book along the perforated lines. Cut out the file-folder label and pocket from page 9. Glue the label onto the file-folder tab. Tape the sides and bottom of the pocket to the front of the folder.

2 Cut out the directions, answer key, and game cards on pages 11 and 13. When the game is not in use, store these items in the pocket on the front of the folder.

3 Cut out the two sides of the game board on pages 15 and 17 and glue them to the inside of the folder.

4 Cut out and assemble the game cube and game markers on page 19.

EXTENDING THE GAME

◎ Give children balloon cutouts. Have them label their balloons with a good-citizen trait. Then have them write or illustrate on the cutouts a way in which they personally demonstrate that trait. Display all the balloons with the title "We Are Filled With Good Citizen Traits."

◎ Ask children to think about a person who deserves a blue ribbon for being a good citizen. Have them design and create a ribbon or other type of award to present to that person. If desired, plan a special class celebration to honor students' selected blue-ribbon citizens.

Blue Ribbon Citizens

GET READY TO PLAY

- Each player places a game marker on Start.
- Shuffle the cards. Stack them facedown on the game board.

TO PLAY

1 Roll the game cube. Move that number of spaces.
Follow the directions on the space.

2 If the space has a blue ribbon take a card.
Read it aloud and keep the card.

3 Keep taking turns. The first player to reach Finish
goes to the BONUS! space. That player takes an extra card.

4 Keep playing until every player reaches Finish.
The player with the most cards is the blue-ribbon citizen for that round.

PLAYING TIP

Players may land on and share the same space.

Blue Ribbon Citizens

ANSWER KEY

Tell the truth.

Stay in line.

Say "please."

Say "thank you."

Use the trash can.

Follow the rules.

Use kind words.

Recycle paper and cans.

Wait your turn to speak.

Return library books.

Clean up after yourself.

Share your toys.

Cross a street carefully.

Use hand signals on
your bike.

Donate to the food bank.

Visit elderly friends.

Help at the animal shelter.

Walk away from fights.

Talk out problems.

Help keep the park clean.

Say nice things to a friend.

Use an indoor voice.

Be polite to others.

Listen and follow directions.

Tell the truth.	Stay in line.	Say "please."	Say "thank you."
Use the trash can.	Follow the rules.	Use kind words.	Recycle paper and cans.
Wait your turn to speak.	Return library books.	Clean up after yourself.	Share your toys.
Cross a street carefully.	Use hand signals on your bike.	Donate to the food bank.	Visit elderly friends.
Help at the animal shelter.	Walk away from fights.	Talk out problems.	Help keep the park clean.
Say nice things to a friend.	Use an indoor voice.	Be polite to others.	Listen and follow directions.

kind

caring

honest

Rude to others. Skip a turn.

START

Bonus!
First player to finish takes a card.

FINISH

Push in line. Go back 1.

friendly

helpful

patient

Return library book on time. Go ahead 1.

Ca

Cut along this edge and attach to page 17.

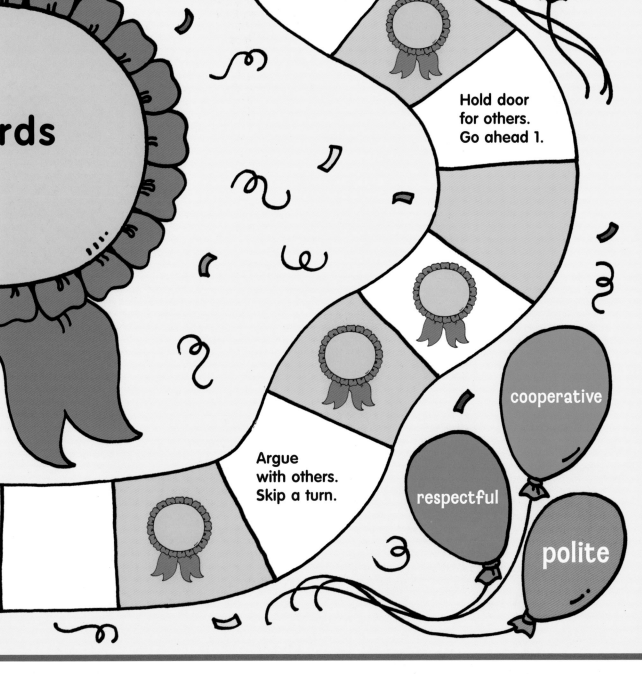

Forget to say "thank you." Go back 1.

responsible

courteous

fair

Hold door for others. Go ahead 1.

rds

cooperative

respectful

Argue with others. Skip a turn.

polite

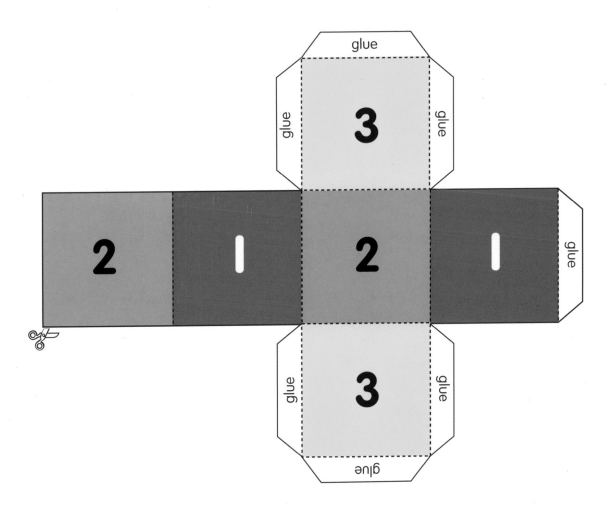

Fold the tabs on the game markers
so they stand up.

Fold here.

Fold here.

Fold here.

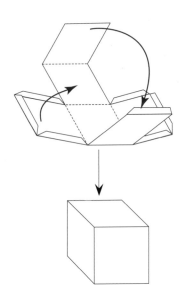

Assemble the cube by folding as shown. Glue closed.

Inside-Out Community

SKILL

This game helps children learn vocabulary related to places and things in the community.

INTRODUCTION

Have children brainstorm a list of places in the community. Write their responses on chart paper. Then read the place name on each game card and have children find that word on the chart. If it is not listed, add it to the chart. Afterward, talk about what kinds of things children might find inside each place.

ASSEMBLING THE GAME

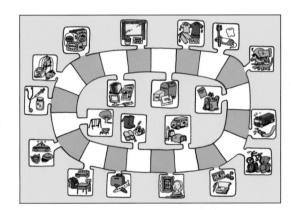

1 Remove pages 23–33 from the book along the perforated lines. Cut out the file-folder label and pocket from page 23. Glue the label onto the file-folder tab. Tape the sides and bottom of the pocket to the front of the folder.

2 Cut out the directions, answer key, and game cards on pages 25 and 27. When the game is not in use, store these items in the pocket on the front of the folder.

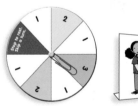

3 Cut out the two sides of the game board on pages 29 and 31 and glue them to the inside of the folder.

4 Cut out and assemble the spinner and game markers on page 33.

EXTENDING THE GAME

◎ Invite children to create a booklet about their favorite places in the community. Have them staple 6–8 sheets of paper between construction-paper covers. Children can draw each of their favorite places on a separate page, including things that are found inside that place.

◎ Form small groups and give a game card to each group. Then invite groups to take turns naming things that are found inside their building. Count how many clues it takes the class to guess the place.

Inside-Out Community

GET READY TO PLAY

- Each player places a game marker on any space on the game board.
- Shuffle the cards. Deal five cards to each player. Stack the rest facedown.

TO PLAY

1 Spin the spinner. Move that number of spaces.

2 Look at the pictures next to the space you land on. Where might you find these things? Do you have a card for that place?

  - If so, place it on the picture box. Then take a card from the stack.
  - If not, your turn ends.

3 After each turn, check the answer key. Is your answer correct? If not, take that card back.

4 Keep taking turns. The first player to get rid of all of his or her cards wins the game.

PLAYING TIPS

- Players may land on and share the same space.
- Players may move around the board as many times as needed.
- When no cards are left in the stack, players continue the game using the cards in their hand.

Inside-Out Community

ANSWER KEY

Left side of game board:

movie theater, grocery store, pet store, doctor's office, police station, school, airport, library, park, shoe store

Right side of game board:

clothing store, dentist's office, zoo, fire station, toy store, bank, museum, post office, restaurant, hospital

Cut along this edge and attach to page 31.

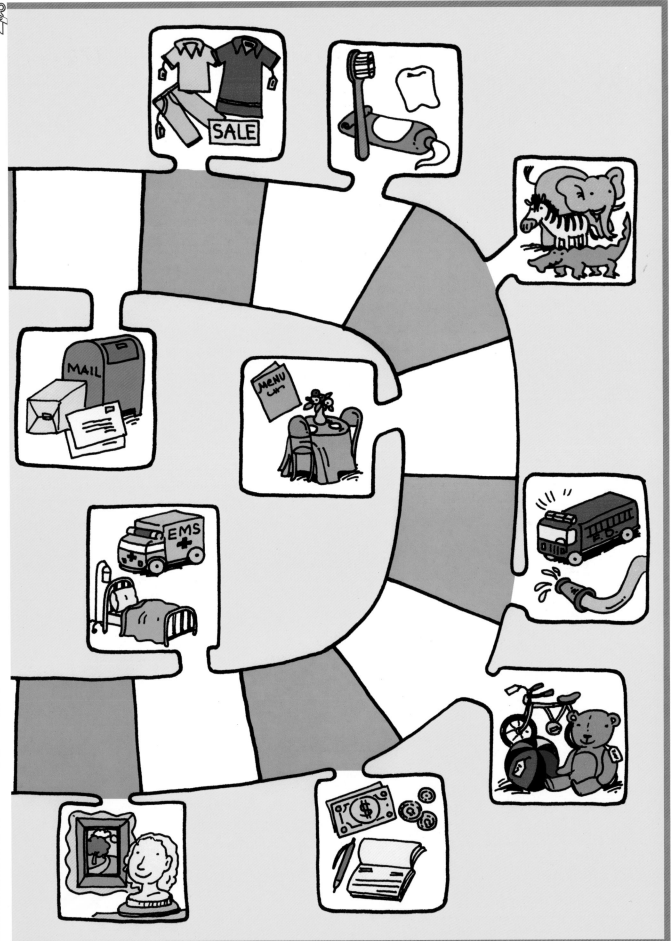

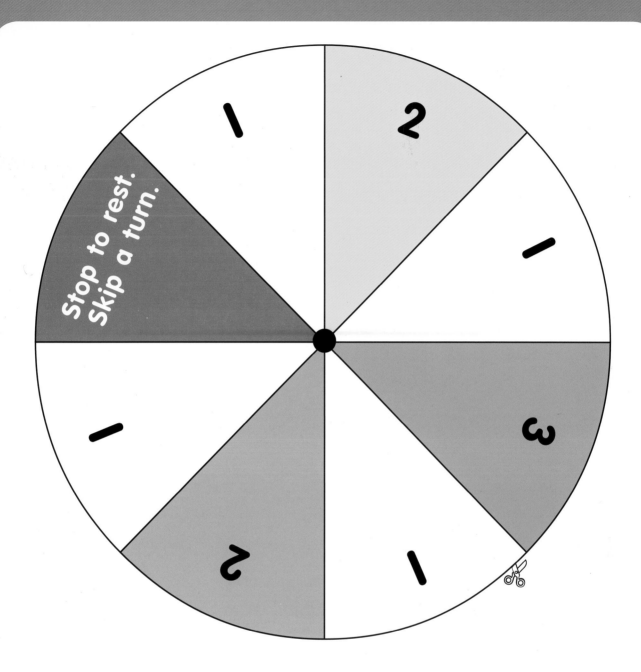

Fold the tabs on the game markers so they stand up.

Fold here.

Fold here.

Fold here.

Fold here.

brass fastener

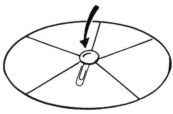

Assemble the spinner using a paper clip and brass fastener as shown. Make sure the paper clip spins easily.

Career Talk

 SKILL This game helps children learn vocabulary related to community workers and their jobs.

INTRODUCTION

Have children brainstorm a list of community workers. Then call out the names of the workers shown on the game board. Add any that are not already on the list. Next, ask students to take turns sharing things that each worker might say while performing his or her job. Afterward, read the sentence on each game card. Challenge children to identify the worker that would say each sentence.

ASSEMBLING THE GAME

1 Remove pages 37–45 from the book along the perforated lines. Cut out the file-folder label and pocket from page 37. Glue the label onto the file-folder tab. Tape the sides and bottom of the pocket to the front of the folder.

2 Cut out the directions, answer key, and game cards on pages 39 and 41. When the game is not in use, store these items in the pocket on the front of the folder.

3 Cut out the two game boards on pages 43 and 45 and glue them to the inside of the folder.

EXTENDING THE GAME

◎ Copy and cut out the community worker pictures from the game board. Put all the pictures in a hat. Pass the hat around from child to child. On a signal, the child holding the hat picks a card, names the worker, and quotes a statement that the worker might say while performing his or her job.

◎ Make an extra copy of the game board and cards. Cut out the community worker pictures and cards. Glue each one to a separate index card. Invite children to play Concentration with the cards, using ten matched pairs for each round.

Career Talk

Career Talk

GET READY TO PLAY

- Each player chooses one game board.
- Shuffle the cards. Stack them facedown.

TO PLAY

1 Take one card from the top of the stack.

2 Read the card. Look on your game board
for a worker who might say this. Do you have a match?

- If so, place the card on the speech bubble for that worker.
- If not, put the card on the bottom of the stack.

3 After each turn, check the answer key. Is your answer correct?
If not, put the card on the bottom of the stack.

4 Keep taking turns. The first player to cover all of the speech bubbles
on his or her game board wins the game.

Career Talk

ANSWER KEY

Game Board 1 (left side):

veterinarian: Your puppy needs shots.

artist: My painting is done.

custodian: I need to mop the floor.

dentist: I will check your teeth.

librarian: Check out your books here.

firefighter: Never play with matches.

cashier: Here's your change.

teacher: It's time for math.

builder: I'll build a house here.

letter carrier: Here's a letter for you.

Game Board 2 (right side):

police officer: Cross the street safely.

chef: Enjoy your meal.

meteorologist: It will rain today.

plumber: The water pipe is fixed.

bus driver: Hop aboard!

hair stylist: Do you want a haircut?

dry cleaner: Your coat is clean.

florist: I have flowers for you.

secretary: I use a computer.

doctor: Take your medicine.

Your puppy needs shots.	My painting is done.	I need to mop the floor.	I will check your teeth.
Check out your books here.	Never play with matches.	Here's your change.	Do you want a haircut?
I'll build a house here.	Here's a letter for you.	Cross the street safely.	Enjoy your meal.
It will rain today.	The water pipe is fixed.	Hop aboard!	It's time for math.
Your coat is clean.	I have flowers for you.	I use a computer.	Take your medicine.

Sign City

SKILL

This game provides practice in recognizing and reading common signs around the community.

INTRODUCTION

Explain to students that signs around the community are designed to help keep citizens informed and safe. Some signs show symbols while others use words. Show children each sign on an enlarged copy of the game board. (You may wish to cut out each sign.) Tell them what each sign means and discuss the symbol, if applicable. Continue by explaining that emergency and service vehicles also use signs to identify them. Then show children the vehicles from the game to identify.

ASSEMBLING THE GAME

1 Remove pages 49–59 from the book along the perforated lines. Cut out the file-folder label and pocket from page 49. Glue the label onto the file-folder tab. Tape the sides and bottom of the pocket to the front of the folder.

2 Cut out the directions, answer key, and game cards on pages 51 and 53. When the game is not in use, store these items in the pocket on the front of the folder.

3 Cut out the two sides of the game board on pages 55 and 57 and glue them to the inside of the folder.

4 Cut out and assemble the game cube and game markers on page 59.

EXTENDING THE GAME

Ask children to make poster-board versions of their choice of signs from the game. Then invite them to set up a pretend community, posting their signs in strategic places throughout the community. Have them role-play different situations that involve reading and obeying the signs.

Sign City

GET READY TO PLAY

- Each player places a game marker on any blank space on the game board.
- Shuffle the cards. Deal five cards to each player. Stack the rest facedown.

TO PLAY

1 Roll the game cube. Move that number of spaces.

2 If the space has a sign, name it. Do you have a matching card?
  - If so, put the card aside.
  - If not, take a card from the top of the stack. Is the new card a match? If so, put it aside. If not, keep the card.

3 After each turn, check the answer key. Is your match correct? If not, take the card back.

4 Keep taking turns. The game ends when a player gets rid of all of his or her cards. The player with the most matching cards wins the game.

PLAYING TIPS

- Players may land on and share the same space.
- Players may move around the game board as many times as needed.
- When no cards are left on the game board, players continue the game using the cards in their hand.

Sign City

ANSWER KEY

Left side of game board:

PARKING	NO U-TURN
AMBULANCE	HOSPITAL
TRAFFIC LIGHT	BICYCLE CROSSING
RAILROAD CROSSING	STOP
U.S. MAIL	PEDESTRIAN CROSSING
YIELD	TRASH CAN

Right side of game board:

BUS STOP	FIRE DEPARTMENT
WALK	DO NOT ENTER
DON'T WALK	TELEPHONE
NO BICYCLES	POLICE DEPARTMENT
ONE WAY	HANDICAPPED PARKING
AIRPORT	SCHOOL CROSSING

POLICE DEPARTMENT	DON'T WALK	WALK	BICYCLE CROSSING
YIELD	NO U-TURN	HOSPITAL	U.S. MAIL
RAILROAD CROSSING	TRAFFIC LIGHT	AMBULANCE	PARKING
BUS STOP	STOP	PEDESTRIAN CROSSING	NO BICYCLES
ONE WAY	FIRE DEPARTMENT	AIRPORT	DO NOT ENTER
TELEPHONE	TRASH CAN	HANDICAPPED PARKING	SCHOOL CROSSING

BUS

rds

FIRE DEPT.

·SCHOOL·

ONE WAY

AIRPORT

DO NOT ENTER

POLICE

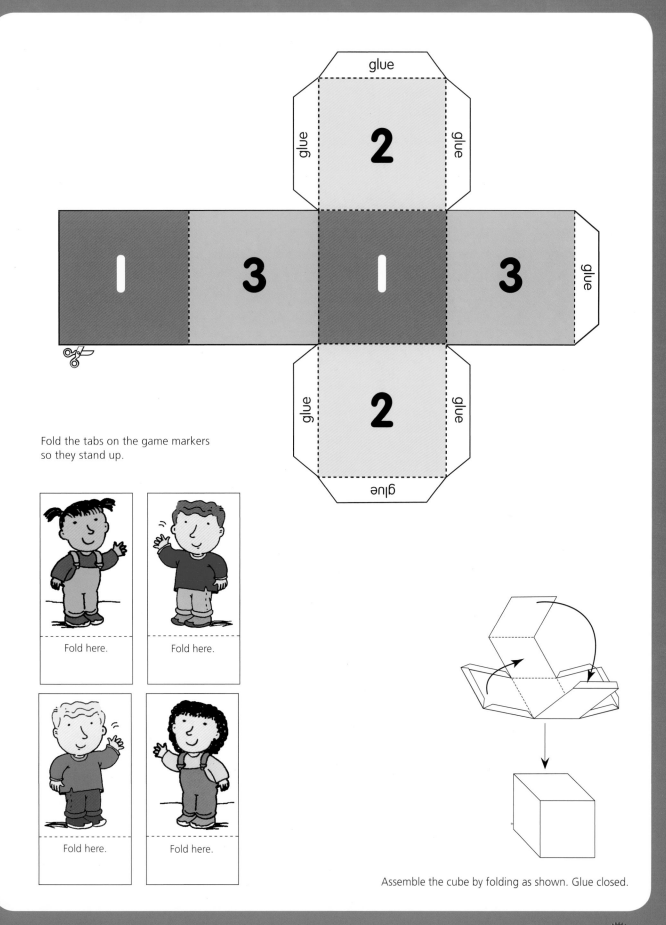

glue

2

glue | glue

1 | 3 | 1 | 3 | glue

glue

2

glue | glue

glue

Fold the tabs on the game markers so they stand up.

Fold here.

Fold here.

Fold here.

Fold here.

Assemble the cube by folding as shown. Glue closed.

Go, Go, Go!

PLAYERS: 2-4

SKILL This game provides practice in recognizing different forms of transportation.

INTRODUCTION

Poll children to find out how they get to school. Do they come by plane, boat, or horse? Explain that, although these may not be daily forms of transportation for them, each one is a means for getting around. Write the forms of transportation already discussed on a chart. Then have students brainstorm others to add to the list. Finally, read the transportation word on each game card. If it is on the list, have a volunteer check it off. If not, add it to the list.

ASSEMBLING THE GAME

1. Remove pages 63–73 from the book along the perforated lines. Cut out the file-folder label and pocket from page 63 Glue the label onto the file-folder tab. Tape the sides and bottom of the pocket to the front of the folder.

2. Cut out the directions, answer key, and game cards on pages 65 and 67. When the game is not in use, store these items in the pocket on the front of the folder.

3. Cut out the two sides of the game board on pages 69 and 71 and glue them to the inside of the folder.

4. Cut out and assemble the number pyramid on page 73.

EXTENDING THE GAME

◎ Copy and cut out an extra set of game cards. Invite student pairs to read the cards and sort them by where they are used: on land, in the water, or in the air. Have them use a copy of the game board to check their work.

◎ Invite children to imagine a day in the city. How many different forms of transportation would they use to get around in the city? Ask them to write and illustrate stories to tell about their transportation adventures.

Go, Go, Go!

GET READY TO PLAY

Shuffle the cards. Stack them facedown.

TO PLAY

1 Roll the number pyramid. Take that number of cards from the stack.

2 Read each card. Then look on the game board.
Can you find a matching picture?

- If so, keep the card.
- If not, put the card on the bottom of the stack.

3 After each turn, check the answer key. Is each answer correct?
If not, put that card on the bottom of the stack.

4 Keep taking turns until all of the cards have been used.
The player with the most cards wins the game.

Go, Go, Go!

ANSWER KEY

Left side of game board:
hot-air balloon, airplane, elevator,
bicycle, stroller, wheelchair, pedestrians,
wagon, subway, taxi, bus, car, van,
truck, horse, rowboat, wave runner

Right side of game board:
blimp, helicopter, push cart, ship,
sailboat, tugboat, train, scooter,
skateboard, in-line skates, RV,
ambulance, motorcycle

airplane	blimp	elevator	stroller	bicycle
wheelchair	pedestrians	wagon	subway	taxi
bus	car	van	truck	horse
rowboat	helicopter	hot-air balloon	ship	sailboat
tugboat	RV	motorcycle	wave runner	train
skateboard	in-line skates	pushcart	ambulance	scooter

Cut along this edge and attach to page 71.

Go, Go, Go! Game Board (right side), page 71

PARK

HOT DOGS

E.M.S.

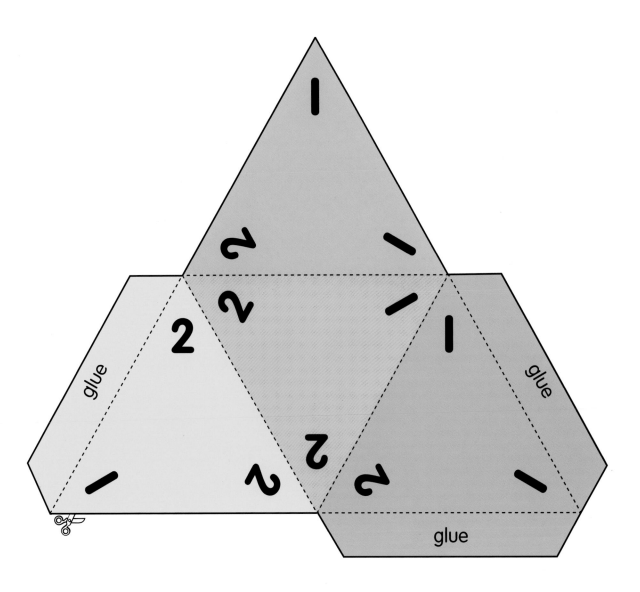

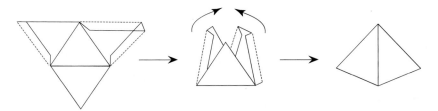

Assemble the pyramid by folding as shown. Glue closed.

Heigh-Ho, the Dairy-O!

SKILL

This game helps children trace the process of how milk gets from the dairy farm to their own homes.

INTRODUCTION

Ask children to share what they know about where milk comes from and how it gets to their homes. Then use the game cards and pictures from the game board to explain the steps that are involved in getting milk from the dairy farm to a person's home. Afterward, help students generate a list of dairy products that can be purchased in a supermarket.

ASSEMBLING THE GAME

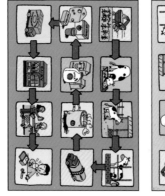
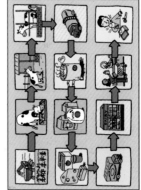

1. Remove pages 77–87 from the book along the perforated lines. Cut out the file-folder label and pocket from page 77. Glue the label onto the file-folder tab. Tape the sides and bottom of the pocket to the front of the folder.

2. Cut out the directions, answer key, and game cards on pages 79 and 81. Store each set of game cards in a separate zipper storage bag. When the game is not in use, store these items in the pocket on the front of the folder.

3. Cut out the two game boards on pages 83 and 85 and glue them to the inside of the folder.

4. Cut out and assemble the number pyramid on page 87.

EXTENDING THE GAME

◎ Invite children to taste-test different kinds of dairy foods. Ask them to secretly write the names of their favorites on separate slips of paper. Then count the slips for each food to find out which one is most popular with students.

Safety Note
Always check for food allergies.

◎ Invite children to take the role of cows. Then call out the name of a food (from any of the food groups). If the food is a dairy product, have the cows "Moo" and swish their imaginary cow tails. If it is not, instruct them to go about their usual cow business, grazing and resting.

Heigh-Ho, the Dairy-O!

GET READY TO PLAY

- Each player chooses a game board and a set of game cards.

- Players spread their cards face up.

TO PLAY

1 Roll the number pyramid.

- Did you roll 1? Find the card that describes the first picture on your game board.

- Did you roll 2? Find the cards that describe the first two pictures on your game board.

Place each card on its matching picture box.

2 On each turn, roll the pyramid. Find the card that matches the next picture, or the next two pictures, on your game board. Place each card on its matching box.

3 After each turn, check the answer key. Is each answer correct? If not, put that card back.

4 Keep taking turns. The first player to cover all of his or her boxes calls out "Heigh-Ho, the Dairy-O!" That player wins the game.

Heigh-Ho, the Dairy-O!

ANSWER KEY

1. The farmer grows grain.

2. Cows eat the grain.

3. Cows go to the milking parlor.

4. Cows are milked twice a day.

5. The milk is put in a special truck.

6. The milk is heated.

7. Some milk is put in containers.

8. Some milk is used for dairy foods.

9. The products go to a supermarket.

10. The products are put out to sell.

11. Shoppers buy the products.

12. Kids enjoy the products at home.

The farmer grows grain.	Cows eat the grain.	Cows go to the milking parlor.	Cows are milked twice a day.
The milk is put in a special truck.	The milk is heated.	Some milk is put in containers.	Some milk is used for dairy foods.
The products go to a supermarket.	The products are put out to sell.	Shoppers buy the products.	Kids enjoy the products at home.
The farmer grows grain.	Cows eat the grain.	Cows go to the milking parlor.	Cows are milked twice a day.
The milk is put in a special truck.	The milk is heated.	Some milk is put in containers.	Some milk is used for dairy foods.
The products go to a supermarket.	The products are put out to sell.	Shoppers buy the products.	Kids enjoy the products at home.

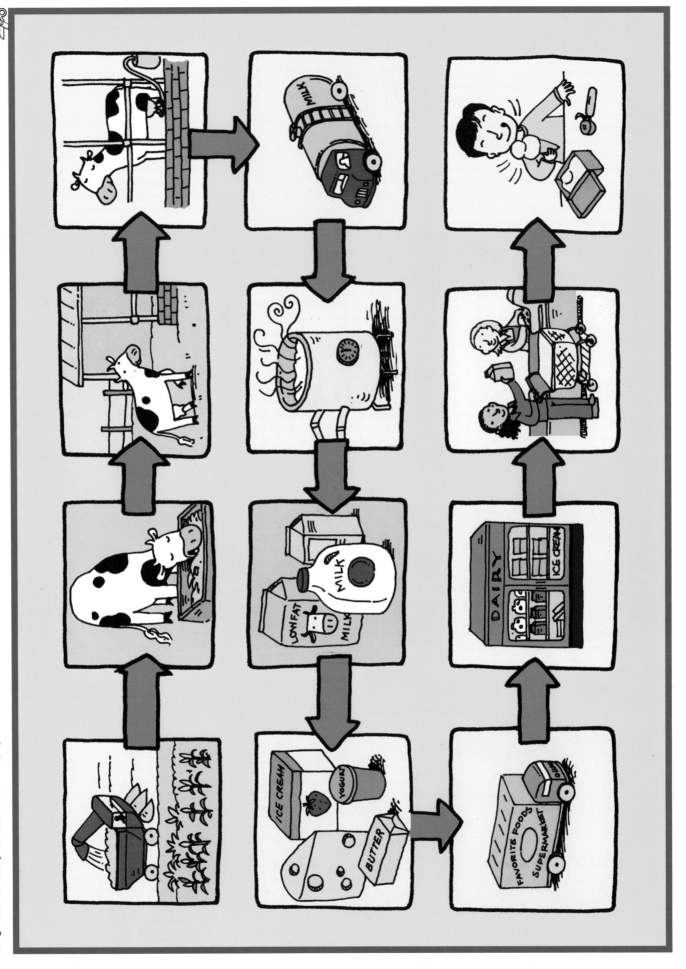

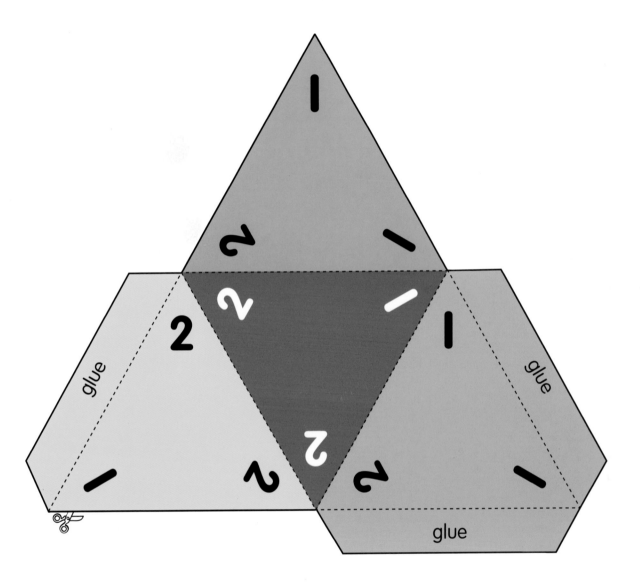

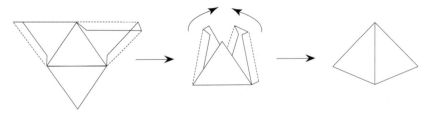

Assemble the pyramid by folding as shown. Glue closed.

Super Seasons, Special Times!

SKILL This game provides practice in recognizing words and concepts related to the seasons of the year.

INTRODUCTION

Write the names of the four seasons on the board. Review with children the word cards associated with each season. Ask them to tell how each word relates to the season.

ASSEMBLING THE GAME

1. Remove pages 91–101 from the book along the perforated lines. Cut out the file-folder label and pocket from page 91. Glue the label onto the file-folder tab. Tape the sides and bottom of the pocket to the front of the folder.

2. Cut out the directions, answer key, and game cards on pages 93 and 95. When the game is not in use, store these items in the pocket on the front of the folder.

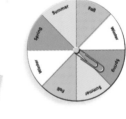

3. Cut out the two sides of the game board on pages 97 and 99 and glue them to the inside of the folder.

4. Cut out the game counters and spinner on page 101. Assemble the spinner.

EXTENDING THE GAME

◎ Copy and cut out the pictures from the game board. Form four groups and assign each group the name of a season. Show the pictures one at a time. When a group identifies a picture belonging to its season, the members stand and call out the season.

◎ Have the four student groups (above) create murals for their seasons. Invite them to use the appropriate picture cards—as well as their own experiences and imaginations—as inspiration for their drawings.

Super Seasons, Special Times!

GET READY TO PLAY

- Shuffle the cards. Deal five cards to each player. Stack the rest facedown.
- Place all of the game counters near the game board.

TO PLAY

1 Spin the spinner. What season does it stop on? Name it.

2 Read your cards. Do you have a card that goes with that season?
- If so, place the card on the matching picture. Take a counter.
  Then take the top card from the stack.
- If not, your turn ends.

3 After each turn, check the answer key. Is your answer correct?
If not, take the card back. Put the counter back.

4 Keep taking turns. The game ends when the stack is empty and
one player has used all of his or her cards. The player with the most
counters wins the game.

PLAYING TIP

Players may play only one card on each turn.

Super Seasons, Special Times!

ANSWER KEY

Fall
first day of school, harvest,
Hispanic Heritage Month,
Columbus Day, Halloween,
Thanksgiving

Winter
Hanukkah, Christmas, Kwanzaa,
New Year's Day, Chinese New Year,
Valentine's Day

Spring
St. Patrick's Day, Passover,
Easter, Earth Day, Mother's Day,
Memorial Day

Summer
Flag Day, Father's Day, 4th of July,
summer vacation, picnic, baseball

first day of school	harvest	Hispanic Heritage Month	Columbus Day
Halloween	Thanksgiving	Hanukkah	Christmas
Kwanzaa	New Year's Day	Chinese New Year	Valentine's Day
St. Patrick's Day	Passover	Easter	Earth Day
Mother's Day	Memorial Day	Flag Day	Father's Day
4th of July	summer vacation	picnic	baseball

Cut along this edge and attach to page 99.

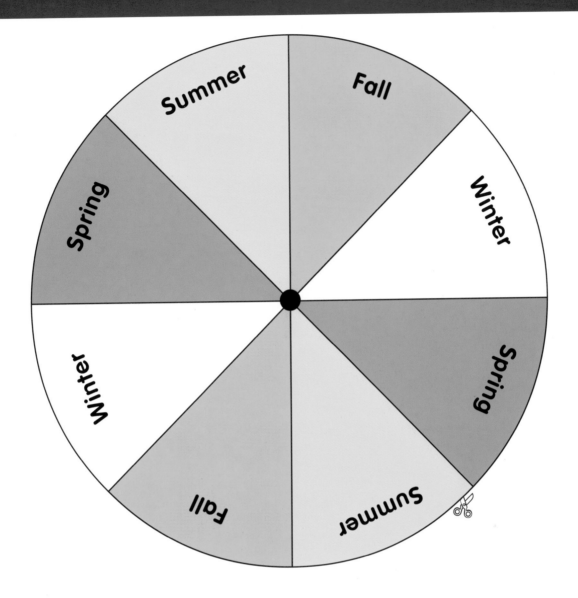

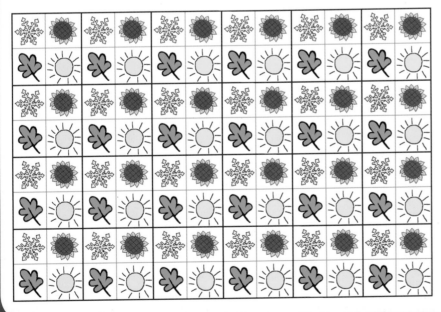

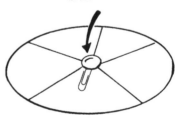

brass fastener

Assemble the spinner using a paper clip and brass fastener as shown. Make sure the paper clip spins easily.

All-American Museum

SKILL This game provides practice in identifying famous American historical figures and national symbols.

INTRODUCTION

List each historical figure and national symbol from the game on the board. Review each one, asking students to tell why that person or symbol is important to Americans. Then read the game cards one at a time. Invite volunteers to identify the historical figure or symbol described by each statement.

ASSEMBLING THE GAME

1 Remove pages 105–115 from the book along the perforated lines. Cut out the file-folder label and pocket from page 105. Glue the label onto the file-folder tab. Tape the sides and bottom of the pocket to the front of the folder.

2 Cut out the directions, answer key, and game cards on pages 107 and 109. When the game is not in use, store these items in the pocket on the front of the folder.

3 Cut out the two sides of the game board on pages 111 and 113 and glue them to the inside of the folder.

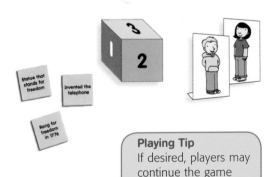

4 Cut out and assemble the game cube and game markers on page 115.

Playing Tip
If desired, players may continue the game until all the cards have been placed on the museum pictures.

EXTENDING THE GAME

Ask children to choose a historical figure or national symbol from the game to research. Have them create illustrated scrapbook pages that tell important or interesting information about their subjects. Compile all the pages into a class book for students to enjoy.

All-American Museum

Abraham Lincoln

All-American Museum

GET READY TO PLAY

- Each player places a game marker on any red space on the game board.

- Shuffle the cards. Deal five cards to each player. Stack the rest facedown.

TO PLAY

1 Roll the game cube. Move that number of spaces.

2 Is your space next to a picture? If so, read the name on it.
Do you have a card that tells about that picture?

- If so, place it on the picture.

- If not, take a card from the top of the stack. Is the new card a match?
  If so, place it on the picture. If not, keep the card.

3 After each turn, check the answer key. Is your match correct?
If not, take the card back.

4 Keep taking turns. The first player to get rid of all of his or her cards wins.

PLAYING TIPS

- Players may land on and share the same space.

- Players may move around the game board as many times as needed.

- When no cards are left in the stack, players continue the game
  using the cards in their hand.

All-American Museum

ANSWER KEY

Squanto: Taught Pilgrims to fish and plant

U.S. Capitol: Where U.S. laws are made

American Flag: Called the "Stars and Stripes"

Harriet Tubman: Led slaves to freedom

Cesar Chavez: Helped migrant workers

Mayflower: Brought the Pilgrims to America

Abraham Lincoln: President who ended slavery

George Washington Carver: Invented uses
for peanuts

Susan B. Anthony: Worked for women's rights

Liberty Bell: Rang for freedom in 1776

Martin Luther King, Jr.: Worked for Civil Rights

Bald Eagle: National bird

Clara Barton: Started the American Red Cross

George Washington: First U.S. President

4th of July: America's birthday

Alexander Graham Bell: Invented the telephone

Sally Ride: America's first female astronaut

White House: Home to U.S. President

Orville and Wilbur Wright: Built and flew first airplane

Statue of Liberty: Statue that stands for freedom

Brought the Pilgrims to America	Taught Pilgrims to fish and plant	Called the "Stars and Stripes"	America's birthday
Rang for freedom in 1776	First U.S. President	National bird	Where U.S. laws are made
Home to U.S. President	Led slaves to freedom	President who ended slavery	Worked for women's rights
Started the American Red Cross	Invented the telephone	Invented uses for peanuts	Statue that stands for freedom
Built and flew first airplane	Worked for Civil Rights	Helped migrant workers	America's first female astronaut

Squanto

U.S. Capitol

American Flag

4th of July

George Washington

Sally Ride

Alexander Graham Bell

Clara Barton

Bald Eagle

Martin Luther King, Jr.

Cut along this edge and attach to page 113.

All-American Museum Game Board (right side), page 113

Harriet Tubman

Cesar Chavez

Mayflower

Statue of Liberty

White House

Abraham Lincoln

Orville and Wilbur Wright

Liberty Bell

Susan B. Anthony

George Washington Carver

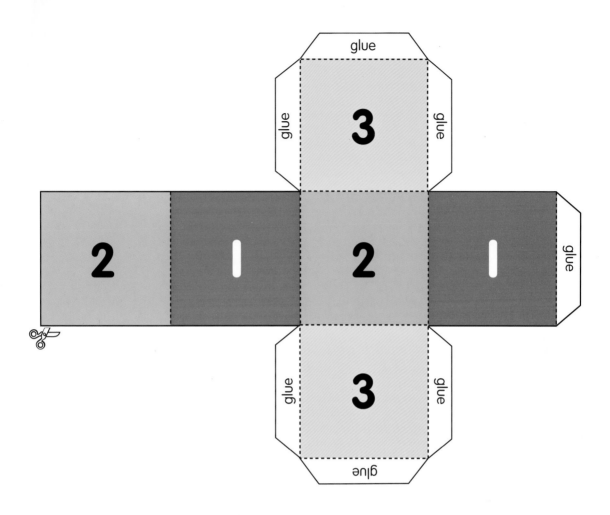

Fold the tabs on the game markers so they stand up.

Fold here.

Fold here.

Fold here.

Fold here.

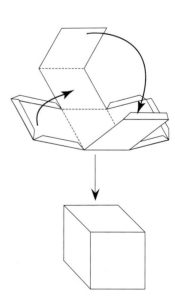

Assemble the cube by folding as shown. Glue closed.

America, Past and Present

PLAYERS: 2

SKILL

This game helps children compare life during colonial times to life today.

INTRODUCTION

Create a two-column chart with the headings "Past" and "Present." Then show children the picture on each game card. Ask them to tell whether the card shows something related to life in the past or life in the present. Have a volunteer stick the picture in the appropriate column on the chart. (You may wish to use reusable adhesive.) After completing the chart, invite students to brainstorm other ways in which life today differs from life in the past.

ASSEMBLING THE GAME

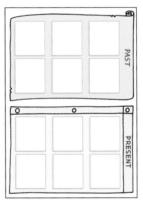

1 Remove pages 119–129 from the book along the perforated lines. Cut out the file-folder label and pocket from page 119. Glue the label onto the file-folder tab. Tape the sides and bottom of the pocket to the front of the folder.

2 Cut out the directions, answer key, and game cards on pages 121 and 123. When the game is not in use, store these items in the pocket on the front of the folder.

3 Cut out the two game boards on pages 125 and 127 and glue them to the inside of the folder.

4 Cut out and assemble the game spinner on page 129.

EXTENDING THE GAME

Ask children to take the role of colonial children. Have them act out a variety of activities common to life as a colonial child. Then have them write about their experiences using feather quills (pencils with feathers taped to them) and aged paper (white paper stained with liquid tea).

America, Past and Present

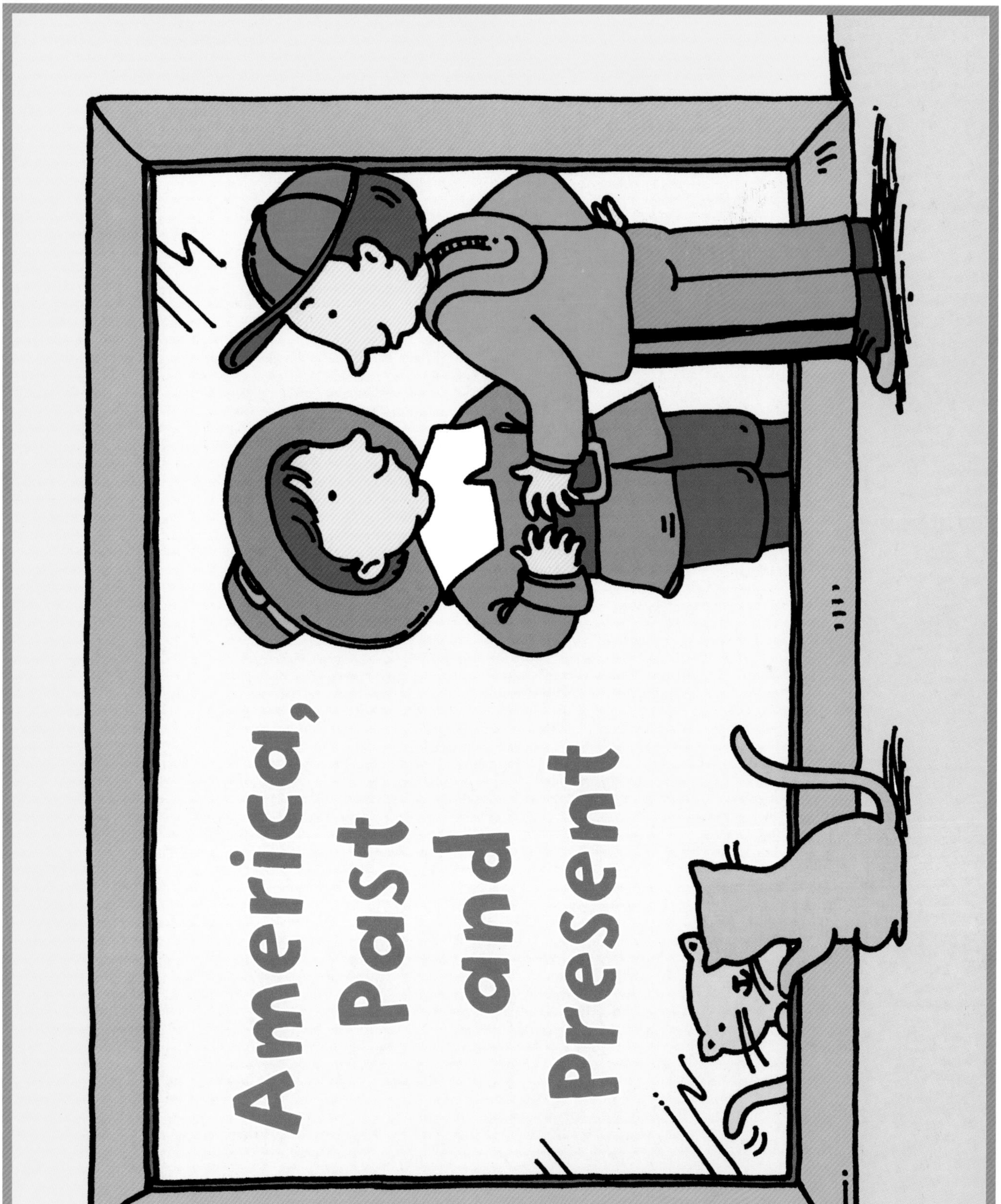

America, Past and Present

GET READY TO PLAY

- Each player chooses a game board.
- Shuffle the cards. Place the stack facedown.

TO PLAY

1 Spin the spinner. Follow the directions.

2 Did the spinner stop on a time period? If so, name it. Then pick a card. Does the picture on the card belong to that time period?

- If so, find that time period on your game board.
  Place the card on a box for that time period.
- If not, put the card on the bottom of the stack.

3 Did the spinner stop on Free Choice? If so, choose Past or Present. Then pick a card. Does the picture on the card belong to the time period you chose?

- If so, place it on a box for that time period.
- If not, put the card on the bottom of the stack.

4 After each turn, check the answer key. Is your answer correct? If not, take the card back.

5 Keep taking turns. The first player to cover all of his or her boxes wins the game.

America, Past and Present

ANSWER KEY

Past

Present

PAST

PRESENT

PRESENT

PAST

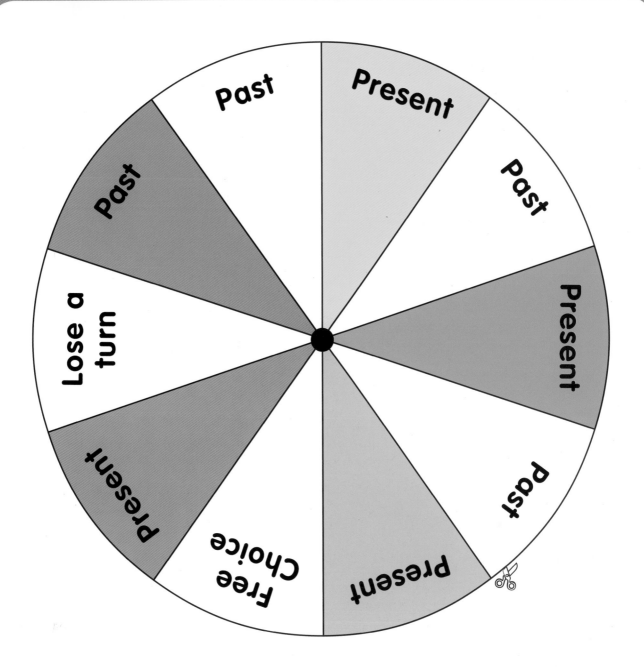

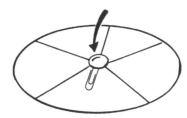

brass fastener

Assemble the spinner using a paper clip and brass fastener as shown. Make sure the paper clip spins easily.

Great Eight State Park

This game helps children learn about different landforms and gives them practice in using map coordinates.

INTRODUCTION

Invite children to name specific landforms they are familiar with, such as local lakes, mountains, and rivers. Then ask them to share what they know about these different landforms. After discussing, use one of the game boards to demonstrate how different landforms might be shown on a map. Point to each symbol on the spinner and invite a volunteer to find a matching landform on the map. As each landform is identified, help children also identify its map coordinates (letter and number pair).

ASSEMBLING THE GAME

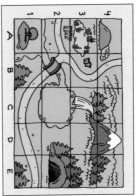

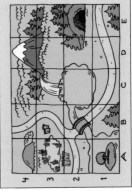

1. Remove pages 133–143 from the book along the perforated lines. Cut out the file-folder label and pocket from page 133. Glue the label onto the file-folder tab. Tape the sides and bottom of the pocket to the front of the folder.

2. Cut out the directions, answer key, and game cards on pages 135 and 137. When the game is not in use, store these items in the pocket on the front of the folder.

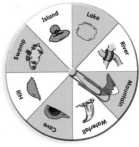

3. Cut out the two game boards on pages 139 and 141 and glue them to the inside of the folder.

4. Cut out and assemble the spinner on page 143.

EXTENDING THE GAME

Have children create maps of their community, state, or a region of the country on large grid paper. Encourage them to develop a key using different colors or symbols to identify different landforms, as well as to label their grid with numbers and letters. When finished, invite children to exchange their maps with partners and then locate different landforms using the map coordinates and the key.

Great Eight State Park

GET READY TO PLAY

- Each player chooses a game board.

- Shuffle the cards. Place three cards face up. Stack the rest facedown.

TO PLAY

1 Spin the spinner. What landform does it stop on?

2 Check the letter and number pairs on the three cards.
Find the matching squares on your game board.
Do any of the squares match the landform shown on the spinner?

- If so, put that card on its matching square.

- If not, your turn ends.

3 If you found a match, check the answer key. Is your answer correct?

- If so, take a new card to replace the one taken.

- If not, put the card back. Your turn ends.

4 Keep taking turns. The first player to cover all eight landforms
on his or her map wins the game.

PLAYING TIP

When no cards are left in the stack, players continue the game
using the cards still in play.

Great Eight State Park

ANSWER KEY

A,1 island   B,2 river   D,4 mountain

A,3 swamp   C,2 lake   E,2 cave

A,4 hill   C,3 waterfall

A, 1	A, 3	A, 4	B, 2
C, 2	C, 3	D, 4	E, 2
A, 1	A, 3	A, 4	B, 2
C, 2	C, 3	D, 4	E, 2

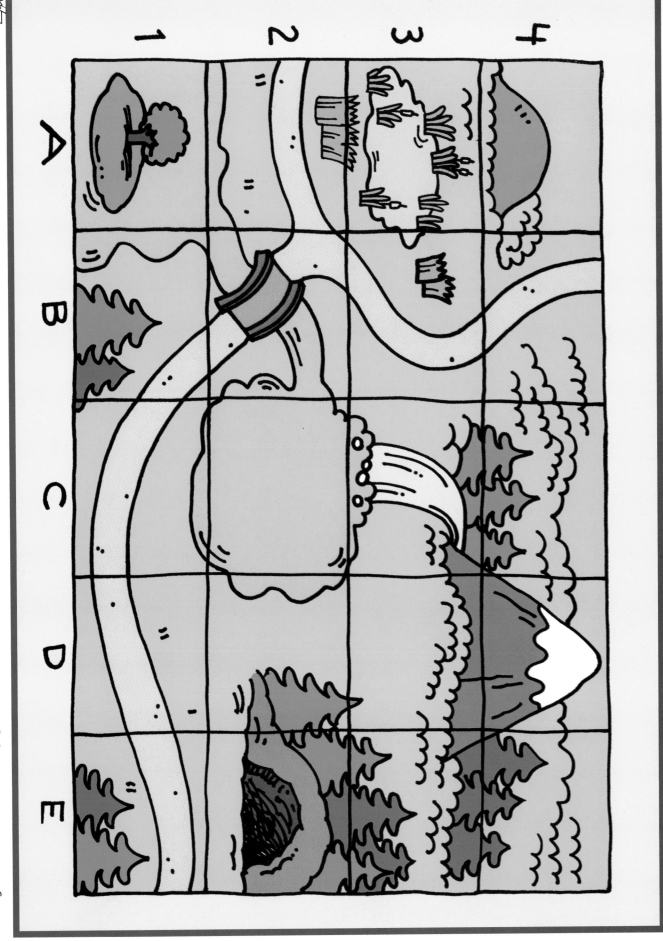

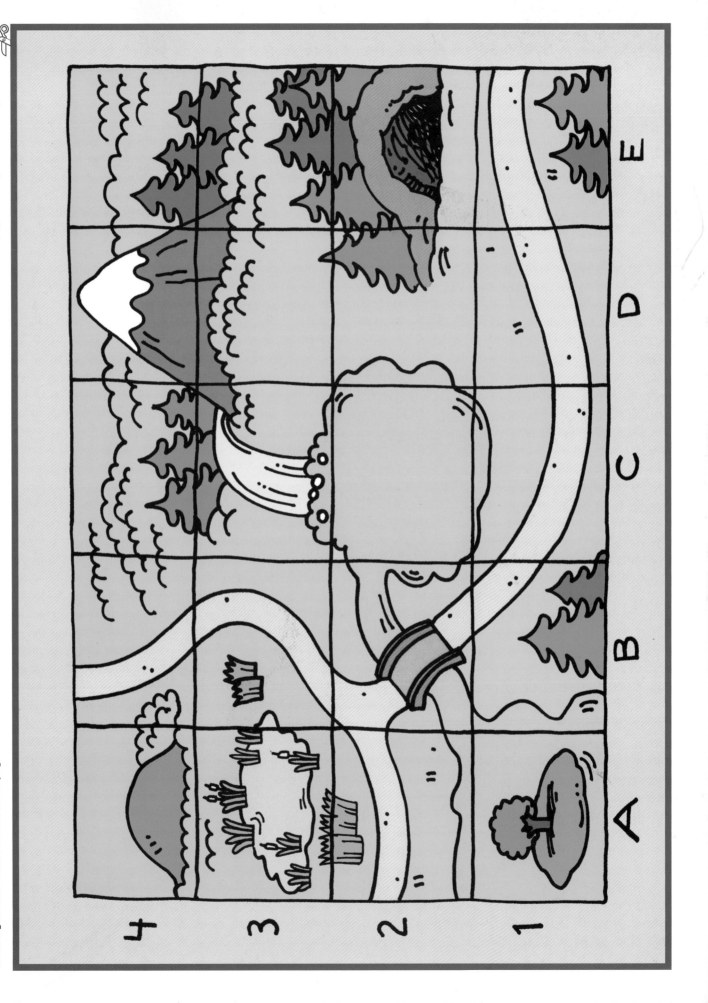

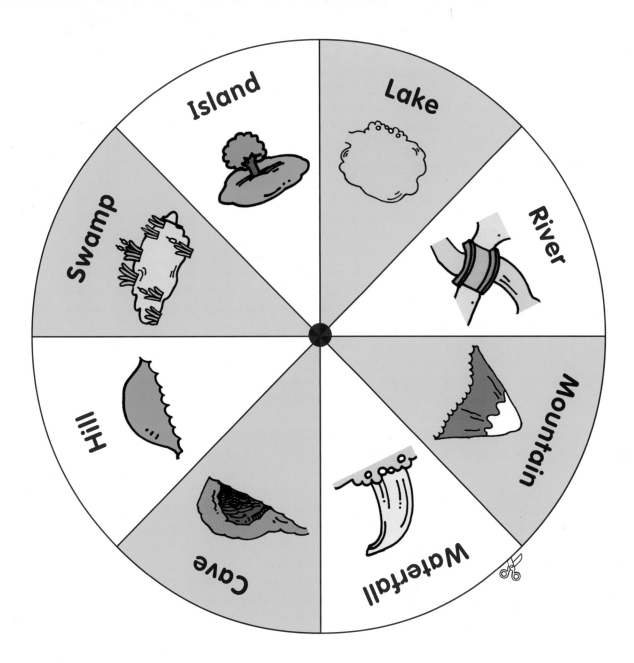

Island

Lake

River

Mountain

Waterfall

Cave

Hill

Swamp

brass fastener

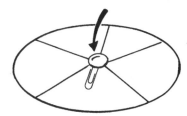

Assemble the spinner using a paper clip and brass fastener as shown. Make sure the paper clip spins easily.